Firefighter

Published in the United States by
QEB Publishing, Inc.
3 Wrigley, Suite A
Irvine, CA 92618

www.qeb-publishing.com

Library of Congress Cataloging-in-Publication Data

Askew, Amanda.
  Firefighter / by Amanda Askew ; illustrated by
Andrew Crowson.
       p. cm. -- (QEB people who help us)
   ISBN 978-1-59566-992-6 (hardcover)
  1. Fire fighters--Juvenile literature. I. Crowson,
Andrew. II. Title.
   HD8039.F5A85 2010
   363.37--dc22

2009001990

Printed and bound in China

Words in bold are explained in the glossary on page 24.

Author Amanda Askew
Designer and Illustrator Andrew Crowson
Consultants Shirley Bickler and Tracey Dils

Publisher Steve Evans
Creative Director Zeta Davies
Managing Editor Amanda Askew

People who help us

Firefighter

Amanda Askew
Andrew Crowson

QEB

QEB Publishing

JAN 2 3 2010

Meet Jack. He is a firefighter.
He helps to make places safe
from fires. He also puts out fires.

Jack arrives at the fire **station**
and he changes into his **uniform**.

At the fire station, Jack wears a blue uniform. When there is a fire alarm, Jack puts on a fire suit, a helmet, and heavy black boots.

His uniform lets people know that he is a firefighter.

Joe, the **Watch Manager**, checks that all six firefighters are there.

First, Jack and the other firefighters have to make sure that everything is working properly when the **alarm** bells go off.

"Everyone's here. Let's start checking and cleaning the truck," Joe says.

Later that morning, Jack fits a
new **smoke alarm** for Mrs. Patel.
He shows her how to use it properly.

"You need to check that it works once a month by pressing this red button. You must also change the batteries twice a year."

"Ok, thanks," Mrs. Patel says.

Jack goes back to the station for lunch.
Just as he's finished his sandwich...
RING, RING, RING!
It's the fire alarm.

Jack and the other firefighters
put on their helmets and rush
to the fire truck.

"Dover Street School.
There's a fire in
the kitchen,"
Joe shouts.

Jack drives and puts on the **siren** so other cars on the road will move out of the way.

When they arrive at the school, the children are standing quietly in the playground. There is smoke coming from the building.

Carl talks to the teacher
to find out what happened.

"Is anyone trapped in the building?"
Carl asks.
"No, all 75 children are out."

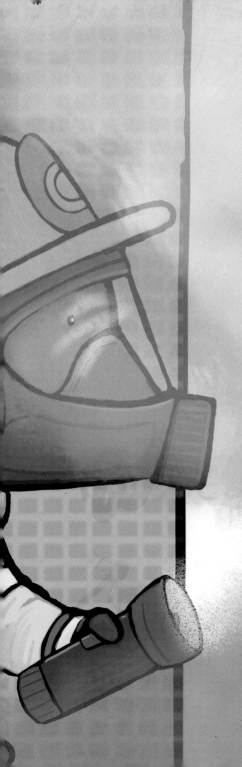

Jack, Peter, and Lucas put
on **air masks** so they can
breathe properly. They crash
through the kitchen doors.

They can hardly see because
the smoke is black and thick.

"Look! It's coming from the ovens." They spray water onto the flames until, at last, the fire is out.

Outside, Jack and Lucas put the hose away.

Peter and Max look to
see what started the fire.
They also check that
the building is safe
before everyone can
go back inside.

21

"Thank you for coming so quickly," the teacher says. "Not a problem!"

Jack feels a tap on his arm. "Please, sir, can we climb on your fire truck?"

Glossary

Air mask Something that covers your face and gives you extra air to breathe.

Alarm Equipment that makes a loud warning noise.

Siren Equipment that makes a loud warning noise. It is usually used on fire trucks and police cars.

Smoke alarm Equipment that makes a loud noise when there is smoke or fire in a building.

Station Place where firefighters work.

Uniform Type of clothing worn by firefighters.

Watch Manager The officer in charge of the fire station and the other firefighters.